Salutes Without Guns

Salutes Without Guns

Ikeogu Oke

First published 2009 by
Manila Publishers,
Flat 22, Block 34,
21, Matadi Street,
Wuse Zone 4,
P. O. Box 10979, Area 10,
Abuja 900001, Nigeria.
Tel: +234-(0)803-453-1501, +234-(0)9-875-1019
Email: info@manilapublishers.com
Website: www.manilapublishers.com

ISBN 978-2436-57-7

To the loving memory of my sister, Eresi,
by whose death I first knew the meaning of deep sorrow.

And to my daughter, Eresi,
by whose birth I first knew the meaning of deep joy.

CONTENTS

A Lyrical Miscellany

Unity Poems

A Cocktail of Epigrams

Acknowledgements

"Circulating Good," "Inspired by Light," "From Now," Gratitude," "That's the Time," "Like Sailors," "Beacons" and "Yellow Beauty" were first published in *Unity Magazine*, the flagship journal of the Unity School of Christianity, Kansas City, Missouri, between September 1988 and November 1999. "Circulating Good" was reprinted in *The Great Sound of Enlightenment* (1989), a book by Hozen Seki, published by the American Buddhist Academy, New York. "From Now" was reprinted in the April 1994 issue of *DISCOVERY*, a magazine published in Braille by the John Milton Society for the Blind, New York. "Fire Report" appeared first in the August 2006 issue of *FARAFINA*, a journal published by Kachifo Limited, Lagos. "Light in Our Tunnel" premiered on April 27, 2004, in the Princess Alexandra Hall of the University of Nigeria, Nsukka, as a special feature of the inaugural Distinguished Lecture of the university's School of Postgraduate Studies. It was first published in *Research and National Development* (2004), a compilation of the proceedings of the lecture by the organizers. "Song of the Gathering Guests" premiered as a special presentation at a dinner organized by the Cross River State Government in honour of a visiting team of UNESCO officials in the Peregrino Hall of the Government House, Calabar, on September 2, 2004. "A Fortnight of Memories" premiered on July 23, 2005, at a reading organized by The Art Republic at the Alliance Française, Enugu. "A 'Savage' Writes Back" premiered on April 26, 2008, in the Princess Alexandria Hall of the University of Nigeria, Nsukka, at a dinner organized by the Association of Nigerian Authors to mark the 50th anniversary of the publication of *Things Fall Apart* by Chinua Achebe. "The Palm wine Ode" premiered on May 23, 2008, in the Vodaworld complex in Gauteng, at a gala dinner organized by the wRite associates, Randburg, to commemorate the golden jubilee of the publication of *Things Fall Apart* by Chinua Achebe. "Epigram on the Nigerian Tiger" was first published in the maiden edition of NEXT newspaper, published by Timbuktu Media Limited, Lagos.

For their roles in the above events, I am grateful to Kadaria Ahmed, Molara Wood, Pamela Yearsley, Philip White, Gérard Chouin, Krydz Ikwuemesi, Muhtar Bakare, Denja Abdullahi, Hyacinth Obumseh, Raks and Sindiswa Seakhoa, Seyoum Bereded, Dr. Ike Achebe, Dr. Ike Okonta, Dr. Wale Okediran, Prof. E. J. Otagburuagu, Prof. S. O. Onyegegbu and Prof. O. C. Enekwe. I also thank Donna L. Miesbach, Paddy Ezeala, Ugochukwu Okoroafor, Nnanna Arukwe, Greg Mbajiogu, Mesembe Edet, Samuel Oyongha, Emeka Agbayi and Dr. P-J Ezeh for their abiding faith; and I thank Chuks Iloegbunam, Lawrence Ani, Akung Jonas, Angus Unegbu, Tony Enyang, James Okpiliya, G. O. Ushie, Awa Samuel, Fidelis Okoro, Enyinnaya Sike, Mature Okoduwa, Dr. J. Elspeth Smith, Dr. Franklin Nwagbara, Dr. Nnadozie F. Inyama, Prof. Kalu Ojah and Prof. A. N. Akwanya for sundry acts of encouragement. I equally thank Jude Nwankwo for writing the music scores for some of the poems in this volume.

I. O.

Preface

The significance of a work of art increases with its having utilitarian value: a beautiful flute, as wood sculpture, will be considered more of the real thing if it produces excellent music in addition to serving as an ornament; and if the music, besides being pleasurable, also has some communicative function, as is sometimes the case in traditional Igbo settings, then its significance as a flute becomes even greater as beauty unites with pleasure and functionality to produce a hybrid of pure and applied art, and a justification of Charles E. Nnolim's assertion that "the value of the work of art transcends its documentary function"[1] which, though made in relation to the folk tradition in African literature, can be said to have wider relevance.

For it is also relevant to the non-literary arts, as I have shown with my example of the [ornamental, musical and communicative] flute; and the principle it encapsulates, that the value of a work of art should have both aesthetical and utilitarian components, is reflected in most of the poems in

---

[1] Charles E. Nnolim, "The Form and Function of the Folk Tradition in Achebe's Novels" in *Approaches to the African Novel* (Owerri: Ihem Davis Press Ltd, 1999) p. 16.

this volume, which more or less assert the inviolability of the aesthetical integrity of art in spite of its having some practical value.

A close look at some of the works in the segment entitled Unity Poems should suffice to justify this claim. For fused with their minimalism and other aesthetical attributes is their inspirational quality whose significance is essentially utilitarian. For instance, the apostrophic tenor of the first ten lines of "Mountaineer" is aesthetical, but it also prepares the ground for the oblique utilitarian exhortation of the concluding six lines:

> Look down and tell
> The ones that come below:
> How high from ground
> The strength of faith can rise,
> What great endurance
> Mounts the rocky heights!

But this dualism of concern, with aesthetics (the ideal of beauty) and utilitarianism (the ideal of functionality, utility or purpose), is perhaps more emphatic in "A Fortnight of Memories," an elegiac sequence which merges significant interests in the aesthetics of form and language with interrogations of the human condition, a manifestation of purpose grounded in social responsibility, thus:

> Have you walked on roads
> Left to fall
> Into disrepair?
>
> Does NEPA mean more light
> Than darkness there?
>
> Have you seen children
> Lost in the maze
> Of vagrancy?

> Have you seen homes
> Covered with mange
> And festering with the sore
> Of poverty?

Then, what I have referred to as the aesthetics of form is evident in the following excerpt from "The Sting of Death," one of the two [Shakespearean] sonnets in the sequence, in which case it is marked by the strict metrical pattern and rhyme scheme that characterize such sonnets, in contrast with the loose form of the preceding excerpts. For instance:

> Tell Apostle Paul that I know where the sting
> Of death is, having been stung by yours
> With a chilliness so deep and so unsparing
> As to cause me pain without a pause.
> …
> Tell him that death's sting is in my heart,
> Whence grave's victory songs infuse my art.

The poem itself is an extended apostrophe, a variant of the conventional apostrophe, which provides a medium for the exploration of what I have characterized as the aesthetics of language, marked in the following excerpt by a slightly veiled repetition and a parallelism of syntax and purport:

> Are there nights
> That walk on tiptoe
> On the grounds
> Of the great beyond?
>
> Are there days so heavy
> They trudge
> On leaden feet?

And if "A Fortnight of Memories" must lay any claim to uniqueness, it is for having transformed the elegy from a medium for expressing profound (and sometimes transcendent) grief, and for plumbing the depths of life and death, to a medium for propagating the type of literature that integrates aesthetical interest with social commitment, as reflected in the penultimate excerpt from the sequence, and in:

> Are there fuel hikes
> Greeted with workers' strikes
> Fuelled by the scarcity
> Of the commodity
> In the midst of high prices
> And soaring inflationary indices?
> Is there such a thing
> As a philosopher king
> Running the affairs of any nation
> To the satisfaction
> Of every citizen
> And every denizen
> In the new world
> Or afterworld
> To which death might have removed
> You from the midst of your beloved
> That you might forever be elusive
> To them — I inclusive —
> Causing a grief
> Of which there can be no end or much relief?

And by "aesthetical interest" I mean such interest that has contrived to rhyme the above lines in pairs, though they flow with the cadence usually associated with free verse, producing a rather hybridised form of poetry which might be referred to as *rhymed free verse*.

Suffice it to say that this tendency to graft purpose to aesthetics is also evident in some of the poems I have assembled as Salutes Without Guns (the eponymous segment of this collection) and A Lyrical Miscellany, though it manifests with a certain peculiarity in "The Palm wine Ode," namely, that I also mean to use the poem (composed on an African subject, and which reflects African sensibilities) to lead the lyric back to its Hellenic roots, when it was required to lend itself to musical performance as an art song and might also have been required to be amenable to being set to music, if the art of musical composition as we know it today were to be in place then, with musical notations and whatnot.

However, only the fraction of "The Palm wine Ode" designated for singing is amenable to being set to music. This is because the poem integrates aspects of the two types of lyrical poetry, namely, the *nominal lyric* and the *full lyric*, in respect of which poems like "A Prayer to My Daughter," "Contemplating Alienism," "Father and Child," "A Prayer to Love" and "Fire Report" exemplify the nominal lyric, while "All Hail Our Alma Mater" and "A Partner in Progress" exemplify the full lyric.

Every poem in this volume is actually a nominal lyric – including those that I have identified as exemplifications of the full lyric, and also "The Palm wine Ode," even in consideration of that fraction of it that can lend itself to musical performance and is amenable to being set to music.

In "The Palm Wine Ode" the nominal-lyric segment, strictly speaking, terminates with the fourth stanza, making way for the full-lyric segment of which the following score is a more or less representative musical fragment[1]:

---

[1] The lines of the fragment, taken from the seventh stanza of the poem, are: Meat was at the ready – salted, peppered, dried. /"He-goat meat," we called it. – It had a stubborn hide. /It lent itself to chewing, with all that taste of brine, /And washing down with pleasure – the night we drank palm wine.

Fragment from "Song of the Palm wine Ode"

Words and Music by **Ikeogu Oke**
Arr with accompaniments by **Jude Nwankwo**

Let me therefore explain that a nominal lyric merely conveys intense feeling or profound thought as is expected of any lyric, whereas a full lyric conveys intense feeling or profound thought *musically*, which explains its characteristic songlike quality, as embodied in poems like Robert Burn's "A Red, Red Rose" and Robert Herrick's "To the Virgins, to Make Much of Time." Also, that the lyricism of a nominal lyric merely approximates to the ideal of impeccable lyricism which verges on musicality and is immanent in every full lyric, and that though a full lyric is necessarily a nominal lyric, a nominal lyric is not necessarily a full lyric, the summary difference being that a full lyric invariably serves as a quarry for or contains the germ of a fluent art song, unlike a nominal lyric.

Indeed, in making these distinctions I am alive to the fact that many a gifted composer can equally derive music from any such lyric that would normally fall into the nominal category, as Beethoven did from Schiller's "An die Freude" (Ode to Joy) and Schubert from Goethe's "Erlkönig" (King).

But music derived from a full lyric will still have an edge over music derived from a nominal lyric – the edge of a naturalness that manifests as a full lyric being recognizable as a song even before it may be set to music, unlike a nominal lyric which becomes a song only after it might have been set to music. In effect, music derived from a nominal lyric is usually *imposed* on the lyric while music derived from a full lyric is normally an intrinsic part of the lyric.

In all, this collection reinforces the balance which I have always tried to maintain between tradition and innovation in my poetry by paying attention to form in both its strict and loose senses, resulting in compositions that may be either rhymed and metrical or not characterized by these attributes, depending on choices which I make intentionally or which I am compelled to make by the inspirational circumstances surrounding the origin of some of my poems. I find it easy to strike such a balance because my Muse and I savour alike the joys of liberty and the wisdom of restraint.

In writing poetry I strive, and shall ever strive, for one thing: the harmony of beauty and sense. And I shall be grateful for my blessing if the reader should find such harmony in the poems assembled in this volume.

Ikeogu Oke
American University of Nigeria, Yola
November 2008

A Fortnight of Memories

(An Elegiac Sequence)

To

Eresi Oke
(1975-2005)

A grief no voice can speak

> I answer the heroic question "Death, where is thy sting?" with
> "It is here in my heart and mind and memories."

> – Maya Angelou, "Death and Legacy"

There is a grief no voice can speak,
Nor mind comprehend;
It cuts deeper than the quick,
And drips pain even after the end.

Such is my grief on the mortal side,
My grief since you died.

You lived life on the wing;
A natural darling,
Never seeking to be loved
To become beloved.

Eternal traveller, teach me not to dread
The spirit of the dead.
Lead me, sister spirit, out of
The void and onto the edge of ethereal love!

Family reunion

The seat where you loved
To sit
Is empty,
Emptier than
The blankness
In our eyes,
And the silence
On our lips.

Father had gone
Before you;
Kalu is aghast,
Like his dreadlocks;
Mother seems stoned:
What can fill the void
When a daughter dies?

Ada, John, Oluchi,
Even I –

You have left a void
That not even love
Nor the fragrance of memories
Can fill,
A void that deepens
With each passing day,
And ever will.

Away but not gone

Away but not gone,
In vain have memories
Tried to fill
The gulf
Of your presence,
Or bridge
The gap
Of your absence.

They come
In long caravans,
Laden with bouquets
And fragrances,
Bearing gifts and banners
Of consolation.

They come with smiles
And eyes that gleam
With hope,
But sigh to see
An ever-widening gulf.

Nights and days

Are there nights
That walk on tiptoe
On the grounds
Of the great beyond?

Are there days so heavy
They trudge
On leaden feet?

Are there rivers
Clogged with dirt
And debris?

Are there men blinded
By the love of lucre?

Are there women
Forced to put work
Before the home
And the cradle?

And what say
Our ancestors
To such things?

Above as below?

Is it really above
As it is below?
Or beneath
As on our
Earthly plane?

Is there Heaven? Hell?
Limbo? Purgatory? – Where are you, my dove[1]?

Are there truly
Such Elysian Fields? – Have you seen father?

Why do the faithful shrink
From the embrace
Of "eternal bliss"?

Why would they rather cling
To the flesh
Even by the thinnest shred
Of their crumbling skin?

What gives
Such honeyed taste
To earthly life?

Have you met believers
Steeped in sin
And the righteous
Who do not believe?

---

[1] Eresi, the name – in my Ohafia (Igbo) dialect – of my late sister
apostrophized in "A Fortnight of Memories," translates as dove.

And what say
Our ancestors
To such things?

The job you needed

Have you found the job
You needed
But could not find here?

Is squalor there the kin
Of opulence?

Does plenty laze about
And scoff at lack?

Does content glory
At the sight of want?

Does labour toil
To fend for indolence?

Are there Nigerian
Sores to a blighted Africa
In the new world
To which you might
Have departed?

And what say
Our ancestors
To such things?

Trees callously felled

Have you seen trees
Callously felled?

Have you walked on roads
Left to fall
Into disrepair?

Does NEPA[1] mean more light
Than darkness there?

Have you seen children
Lost in the maze
Of vagrancy?

Have you seen homes
Covered with mange
And festering with the sore
Of poverty?

Have you walked on streets
Paved with vice?

Have you been
To neighbourhoods
Where crimes breed
Like vermin?

---

[1] NEPA: acronym for National Electric Power Authority, Nigeria's electricity industry, reconstituted as Power Holding Company of Nigeria (PHCN) in June 2005.

And what say
Our ancestors
To such things?

Calluses and power

Have you noticed calluses
Hardening around the heart
Of power?

Are there hordes
Of listless youth
Whose future
Has been squandered
By misrule?

Are there drugs in search
Of hospitals and hospitals
In search of drugs?

Have you witnessed wars
Fuelled by lust and greed?

Have you seen parents
Whose children lie supine
In the bog of despair?

And what say
Our ancestors
To such things?

Hikes and strikes

Are there fuel hikes
Greeted with workers' strikes
Fuelled by the scarcity
Of the commodity
In the midst of high prices
And soaring inflationary indices?
Is there such a thing
As a philosopher king
Running the affairs of any nation
To the satisfaction
Of every citizen
And every denizen
In the new world
Or afterworld
To which death might have removed
You from the midst of your beloved
That you might forever be elusive
To them – I inclusive –
Causing a grief
Of which there can be no end or much relief?

The Sting of Death[1]

"O death, where is thy sting? O grave, where is thy victory?"

— 1 Corinthians 15:55 (KJV)

Tell Apostle Paul that I know where the sting
Of death is, having been stung by yours
With a chilliness so deep and so unsparing
As to cause me pain without a pause.
Tell the great Apostle that I – even I –
Now hum the victory song of the grave
That hides your easy charms from earth and sky
As though in a deep, sand-stuffed, impenetrable cave.
O that he knew that the promise of resurrection
Does not remove the potent sting of death,
Nor does the hope of bliss without cessation
Annul our loss when robbed by the grave on earth.
Tell him that death's sting is in my heart,
Whence grave's victory songs infuse my art.

---

[1] This sonnet and the subsequent one are so closely related that they may
be regarded as complementary. Both are recommended for reading in a
tone so elegiac as to resonate with the kind of ponderous solemnity that
Alexander Pope suggests in lines 370-371 of Book II of "An Essay on
Criticism," that is, "When Ajax strives some rock's vast weight to
throw,/The line … labours, and the words move slow."

The Victory of the Grave

"O death, where is thy sting? O grave, where is thy victory?"

– 1 Corinthians 15:55 (KJV)

If the hope of eternal bliss does not annul
The pain of bereavement, wherefore, then,
Does death not sting or is grave not victorious at all –
Over us: as yet the earthbound, mortal sons of men?
If the promise of resurrection does not void
The agony of separation with our loved
Ones, why, then, must we – mere mortals – avoid
Admitting grave's victory over us and our beloved?
Is a sting effaced by a pain that proves to be brief?
Or a victory not its kind for being short-lived?
Brief may be the earthly span of our grief;
Does that belie their anguish who have grieved?
Please pose these questions to Apostle Paul;
To the great Apostle pose them one and all.

Your picture still stands on the wall

Your picture still stands
On the wall next to father's
And on the shelf
By itself.

Who can bear
To bring them down,
Though they stir
Our common pool
Of grief?

One smiling,
The other
Coruscating with cheer,
Who can bear
To bring them down?

Who can wish away
Your joyful eyes,
Even for the loss
They call to mind?

The grief I have known

There is a grief
That weighs
Like lead
Against the heart,
Like stone
Against the tongue,
That hangs
Like stormy clouds
Above the mind,
A dumb
And helpless grief
For all its rage,
That stiffens thought
And poisons
The blood
With bile.

Worse is the grief
I have known
Since the day
You died.

Mma Nnekwu[1]

Our mother's mother's hair
Has turned white
Like wood ash;
Her gait is twice
As wrinkled
As her stoop;
She has tottered
Like a child
And prattled
In her sleep
Since the wake
Of that benighted day.

Nor can she say adieu!

---

[1] *Mma* Nnekwu – in my Ohafia (Igbo) dialect – would translate as "Materfamilias Nnekwu," Nnekwu being the name of my maternal grandmother, evoked in the first line of the stanza as "mother's mother's" – a transliteration of *nne nne* (Igbo for maternal grandmother).

Salutes Without Guns

"Salute Silhouettes" by Joshua Theophilus/Adams Gbolahan

Epigraph

I raise a clenched fist
In salutes without guns,
To lives who, seeking glory,
Eschew violence.

I touch my beaming face
In salutes without guns,
To lives who, seeking honour,
Take the path of peace.

I blow a squelching kiss
In salutes without guns,
I blow a kiss to them
In civil, warm salute.

A "Savage" Writes Back

(To Chinua Achebe[1]: On reading his comments on V. S.
Naipaul's contempt for the African in *Home and Exile*)

Evil is never ameliorated
by being tolerated.
It only grows worse,
like the cancer of the imperial curse
that invades the mind of its victim
and decimates to nought his self-esteem.

But need we worry about V. S. Naipaul[2]
or lose sleep to an ever-fawning doll?
A slave, glorified, remains a slave,
a grave-
       digger in Her Majesty's service, making words his spade,
hurling insults over his own head.

Does it improve a slave that the chains
have left his wrists for his brains,
the manacles
his ankles
for his heart, that his soul
has derailed into a mole
bumbling all its days
in the sun's rays,
unable to see evil for what it is,
that a world unjust is twice amiss?

---

[1] Chinua Achebe: a Nigerian novelist, essayist and poet.
[2] V. S. Naipaul: a Trinidad-born novelist and essayist; he was awarded the 2001
Nobel Prize in literature.

Light in Our Tunnel

(For Dora Akunyili[1])

Yet, for her good works and fruitful pains,
I can say for our nation: the glory remains[2].

Let us rejoice for the light in our tunnel.

Let us rejoice though we may yet find an end to the tunnel.

Let us rejoice though at that end we may know the
    luminescence of more light.

Let us rejoice for the bounty of this light
whose tongue licks the darkness away from inside our tunnel.

Without such light how can we find our way?
The bumbling moles we would rather be, trapped in a
    subterranean isle,
pulling triggers when we should be offering sacrifice of praise
for the light in our tunnel.

Night, more lame than Vulcan[3], labours at his forge,
A looming presence like a demiurge.
What gloom must flow to us from his runnel
Of rock but for such a rare light in our tunnel!

---

[1] Dora Akunyili: a Nigerian Professor of Pharmacology who served as
the Director of NAFDAC (acronym for National Food and Drug
Administration and Control), a Nigerian federal parastatal, and is
currently Nigeria's Minister of Information.
[2] The glory remains: a translation of "Permanet Gloria," the title of a sonnet
by the French poet Pierre de Ronsard (1524-1585).
[3] Vulcan: the god of fire in Roman mythology.

A tunnel in a dead volcano, a darkness inscrutable
but for this light whose warm tongue licks away the icy gloom
from our winding crypt, our tunnel.

What gloom but for such light, gentle but perseverant, and calm
with a bright-tongued flame, lapping up the darkness streaming
into this damp hole, this stuffy place, this tunnel, refusing
to be put out by the shrapnels of spite and the squalls of
        ingratitude.

Should they not have prayed for the life of this light,
though stiff at heart and exiles from the realm of thankfulness,
and prayed for more lights like her at the end of our tunnel?

Should they not have prayed for her life who share our tunnel
though they may not know it, and who like the rest of us
may forever grope in the dark but for a light like hers?

At the Foot of the Lamido

A willing bond, a grateful guest,
I sat at the foot of the Lamido – the Lamido
Who saved my people from a raging mob
Before the war[1].

I went with a son of one of those my people[2]
And sat at the foot of the Lamido.

He had kept the raging mob at bay, a mob
Thirsty for the blood of innocents, kept the mob at bay
As he shepherded the flock of my people
Into his royal sanctuary.

He had kept the barking mob at bay, a mob
Hungry for the flesh of innocents, kept the mob at bay
As he shepherded the flock of my people
Into his royal sanctuary.

And yet at bay he kept the mob
As, sheep by sheep, he led the flock of my people
To a boat to sail home to safety
On the back of the Benue[3].

And forty years thence I went with the son
Of a man in that flock
And sat at the foot of the Lamido.

---

[1] The Nigerian Civil War (1967-1970).
[2] A son… people: Okey Ndibe, a Nigerian academic, writer and journalist, with whom I visited the Lamido of Adamawa, Dr. Aliyu Musdafa, in his palace on July 7, 2008.
[3] River Benue, Nigeria's second biggest river.

He said Islam forbids the shedding of innocent blood;
He said all religions forbid the shedding of innocent blood;
And yet he said he saved those lives for its sheer rightness;
That he would still have saved them even if Islam and other
        religions
Do not forbid the shedding of innocent blood.

And we listened with grateful hearts
As I sat at the foot of the Lamido,
The Lamido Aliyu Musdafa,
The Lamido of Adamawa.

And we are humbled by humanity and never by the growls
        of power,
And we are subdued by compassion and never by the snarls
        of power,
And we are drawn to kindness and never to the spoils of
        power.

And we are edified by the benevolence of the good Lamido.

So Long as Our Candle Burned

(To John Kerry[1] – and all Democrats)

I

In Enugu, city of coal and mouldering hills,
City of The Rising Sun, where the dawn wakes
In silence and ascends the sky
In plumes of mist,
There is a place called The Chancery,
Where Arthur Nwankwo[2] holds court,
An Upper Room of no Last Supper,
A sanctuary of minds and their treasured gifts,
A room valued more by its habitués
Than they value sunshine
Who live in Arctic climes.

That was where we sat – a ring
Of ten men round a bright candle –
And waited for that victory that finally
Slipped by. We would not relent
So long as our candle burned.

Together we sat, keeping vigil
Through a long long night, our hearts
Fluttering like the flame on the tip
Of that lone candle whose light
Betokened the fresh hope
You were to bring
With a bright new dawn.

---

[1] John Kerry: a US Senator and candidate of the Democratic Party in the 2004 US Presidential election.

[2] Arthur Nwankwo: a Nigerian intellectual, politician, and publisher.

And twice a tyrant cold congealed the air;
Yet we would not relent
So long as our candle burned.

What could we have said to fate
If you had not fought a good fight?
The soaring eagle of three tough debates!

Could we have said
That success is ever deserved?
Or failure ever shameful?
That the race is always for the nimbler foot?
Or triumph always for the nobler soul?

Now you exhort that it is time
To reunite your dear country
And heal her broken bones
With the balm of truth
And loving kindness, values
Long sidelined before
You would emerge
And strive to win for change,
Only to become nobler
And more dear to us
Even in defeat!

We have taken heart.

II

Democrats, defenders of true freedom and world peace,
Believers in the dignity of all beings and nations,
Our fortress may be embattled but shall never be conquered.
It shall never be conquered!

The Muse of Criticism

(For Charles E. Nnolim: In remembrance of our
conversation on the significance of the critic and after
reading his *Approaches to the African Novel*)

She's the Muse
Not reckoned with the daughters of Zeus.
She should be one of them,
And wear like them a laurel diadem:
A worthy sister of the virtuous nine,
The closest kin to share their state divine;
A feted being-divine amid their ranks,
Like the nine deserving of our thanks.

She it is that makes their virtues shine,
That gleans their works for purpose and design;
She the fluid and ever-roving bridge
That links their labours to their due prestige.

---

[1] Chalres E. Nnolim: a Nigerian literary critic and Professor of Literature.
[2] Daughters of Zeus: the nine goddesses, or Muses, in Greek mythology,
born of the god Zeus and Mnemosyne, the goddess of memory, and
believed to inspire all artists, especially poets, philosophers, and musicians. –
Paraphrased from "Muses." Microsoft® Student 2007 [DVD]. Redmond,
WA: Microsoft Corporation, 2006
[3] The Muses are usually depicted as wearing crowns made from laurel leaves,
and the leaves are regarded as sacred to them.

Yes, she's the Muse of the art of elucidation
Whose labours win for art its best devotion.
Nor should she ever be far from the Graces[1],
That lend their ageless charm to joyous places.

Or what would art be without criticism?
A dazzling trumpet with a muffled sound!

---

[1] The Graces: the three goddesses, in Greek mythology, born of the god
Zeus and the nymph Eurynome, who, as regular companions of the Muses,
presided over dances, banquets, and all other pleasurable social events, and
brought joy and goodwill to both gods as mortals. – Paraphrased from
"Graces (Greek goddesses)." Microsoft® Student 2007 [DVD]. Redmond,
WA: Microsoft Corporation, 2006.

A Night in Midrand[1]

(To Raks Morakabe Seakhoa[2])

You have gathered us
For a night of the fiddle.

Gauteng burns,
And we're no courtiers of some modern Nero[3].

Yes, you have called us
To assert the superiority of culture to savagery,
Of love to hate,
Of art to guns, spears and cudgels – all the paraphernalia of
    violence –
And of the bright candle of goodwill
To the sooty flames of arson.

You have called us to pray for the soul of your dear land
In her hour of tribulation,
And burn the incense of hope
On this night of wanton ruin.
And its fragrant smoke ascends the sky!
And see its fragrant smoke ascend the sky!

We have come with voices called blessed by the Muses;
The poets of South Africa have sung to their fill
And mourned to the limits of all distress;
They have called down the Graces to this night of drinks and
    dirges,

---

[1] Midrand: a suburb of Gauteng, a province in South Africa.
[2] Raks Morakabe Seakhoa: a South African culture activist.
[3] Nero (AD37-68): the Roman emperor notorious for playing the fiddle while
Rome was being razed by an inferno.

This mournful bacchanal.

Yet no land of plenty
Should watch her chicks mourn for hunger
Or thirst at the trough.

Or what is *ubuntu*[1]?

---

[1] Ubuntu: humanity, goodness, and compassion, regarded as fundamental to the African approach to life; the word originates from South Africa, where it is more or less synonymous with kindness.

Lest We Forget

(To Chimamanda Ngozi Adichie[1]: On reading *Half of a Yellow Sun*[2])

Their votes no longer count
In the land they fought us
To keep as one,
In the land for whose unity
They slaughtered us;
And it's barely
Forty years
Since then.

Lest we forget.

How things have changed!
But who can tell
Whether for the better,
Or worse?

Those who killed us like flies
Now fear for their lives;
Those who plugged our throat
With pain
Now have the gag-man's nozzle
To their skull;
A sulphur stench of terror fills our land;
A monster of dread reigns over our shrunken lives[3].

---

[1] Chimanada Ngozi Adichie: a Nigerian writer.
[2] Incidentally, this poem had gone into circulation before Adichie was awarded the Orange Prize for *Half of a Yellow Sun*, her second novel.
[3] The stanza alludes to the political situation in Nigeria at the time of publication of *Half of a Yellow Sun*.

Time does not heal wounds inflicted with forethought.
I defy her to heal this for I know she cannot,
This wound of pogroms from which flows the pus of Biafra,
From whose gash flowed too much innocent blood
To stain the soul of our yet-benighted land.

The Race

(To Chimalum Nwankwo[1])

Athlete and light bearer,
Could you bring the flame ever nearer
That is dancing on the brand
In your right hand?

See, the night
Engulfs my sight
And the track on which I run
With my back to the hours of the sun.

I have run past the red flag of dusk;
Around me odours lay foul claims to musk;
And a stray scent brings to my nose
A faint hint of some ever-distant rose.

The rest of my track winds up a smoky hill
The thought of whose steepness makes my breath stand still;
Yet I must continue to run
With or without the sun.

---

[1] Chimalum Nwankwo: a Nigerian poet and academic.

The Master Builder

(To Chima Ubani[1]: A Graveside Salute)

We know what you lived for;
We know why you died,
Master builder.

Our bricks were made of dust,
Our mortar of wind;
Our castle hung limply in the air,
The castle of our dreams for a just and civil rule.

Then you arrived,
Dredging substance from the sea of thought,
That our castle may stand on solid ground.

We know what you lived for;
We know why you died,
In life we knew you well,
And have known you better in death,
Master builder.

You leave behind a horde of splintered lives,
Voices to be hushed forever to silence,
Hearts lost irretrievably in the maze of grief,
A nation almost doomed.

Master builder,
Will your light so shine before us
That we, groping hearts, fumbling hands,
Minds long lost in dark, nocturnal alleys,

---

[1] Chima Ubani (1963-2005): a frontline Nigerian civil rights activist.

May see our labours at a glorious end?

Will it, the gentle light of your luminous grace,
Shine upon us from the firmament?
Will your resilience abide with us?

Shine, gracious light, shine upon us yet,
Builders in the land you lived and died for,
Lest it become truly doomed in spite of your labours,
Lest we and our land be truly doomed.

Our hopes flee faster than we can give chase;
The night closes in upon us.
Beam your gentle light upon us,
Master builder.

Our hopes flee faster than we can give chase;
The minions of darkness creep out upon us,
Laying deadly mines across our path,
Master builder.

Beam your light upon us that we may yet see;
Breathe within us that we may stay the course;
Master builder, transformed presence, dwell among us yet;
May your gentle strength abide with us!

In the Wake of Your Interment

(To Kalu Udo Uma[1])

I did not know you.
I am merely your kinsman.

But then I am no bearer of cautionary tales,
The son, I must say, of my father.

I pull back from my grief and look at your bright obituary:
The tasselled cap,
The bright gown, the hood,
The striped long tie that girds a white collar.

I look at the glint in those eyes,
At that look cast proudly at the horizon,
Straining at glories that might have known no bounds.

I look most of all at the perfect "V" of that smile
That asserts a scholarly chin,
And wonder that fate could so do us in,
The children of Ugwuonyiriegbe[2],
So do us in!

And how could I have stood
This sight of sunlight in a casket?
I whose eyes still brim with tears!

---

[1] Kalu Udo Uma (1956-2003): a Nigerian geologist and academic.
[2] Ugwuonyiriegbe (translation: the gun-defying hill): a sobriquet for my hometown, Akanu Ohafia, which probably originates from its ring of hills having served as a sanctuary from the federal troops during the Nigerian Civil War.

A Bud of Light

(To Nwojo Agwu[1])

I have known nights
When the sky opened
And drenched my gloomy
Soul with bitter rains.

And the dawn broke
With golden rays
From the same sky
And dried me.

I have known the hidden pits
Of quiet aggression,
On selfsame grounds
Where love has kept me safe.

I have known
The cheerful prowl of jealous foes
And the smiling snares
Of envious rivals.

I have also known friends and mentors
Who will not brook
A shield above my light.
Many bright pearls of humanity!

And I have learnt to keep faith
Even in gardens of darkness;
For I know that buds like you
Will burst with light!

---

[1] Nwojo Agwu: a Nigerian mathematician and academic.

As I Celebrate

(To Barack Obama[1])

Ever shall the echo of your victory circle the earth
And bring fresh hope to all despairing souls.

And your feat has roused the hopes I nurse for my country
Trapped in the labyrinth of infamy.

That she should awaken, the giant she's deemed to be,
And learn to give faith to her teeming young.

That she should tend the dreams of those young
And lead them to that clime where honour reigns.

That the aged who are hers may join to give
Good nurture to those dreams
And come to live free from all fear and want.

And that she should be a beacon of a land
Where power rests with merit and with truth.

O that I could see the dawn of these hopes
Lit by the iridescent flame of her rebirth
In the light of your dream victory!

I mourn her grim plight as I celebrate.

---

[1]Following his election as the first African-American President of the
United States.

Ode on the Night of the NEXT[1] Launch

(For Dele Olojede[2])

The sun is ever rising,
Climbing the dim slope of our dark despair,
Toiling upwards, heavenwards.

Like this one – which rose,
Not like the earthly sun
At the stroke of dawn,
But like an ethereal sun
At the antipode of noon,
At midnight.

And may the spirit of excellence
Ever dwell among us who saw
The midnight dawn of its ascent,
Who stayed awake to see its rays emerge.

And I have looked at the mountaintop
Where its rise shall only begin,
And I can see that its light is splendid!

---

[1]NEXT: a Nigerian newspaper launched (on the internet) by midnight
on December 19, 2008.
[2]Dele Olojede: a Nigerian journalist and publisher of NEXT who won
the 2005 Pulitzer Prize for International Reporting.

A Lyrical Miscellany

A Prayer for My Daughter

Tomorrow the neighbours
Will gather for your naming,
And the moon and stars
Will await their turns
To pay you obeisance,
My radiant one!

May your life like theirs
Be bright
Even in the hours of darkness.

May your road not be smooth
With the smoothness
That slackens the limbs of the mind
Or rough with the roughness
That inclines the soul to despair.

In the worlds' welter of winding ways
May you find the middle path
To decent glory
And the wisdom and courage
To take to it
Though it were massed with rocks.

May you not know valleys
Without mountains,
Or fortune without labour,
Or forget that life is a gift
To be earned through service.

May you know the peace
That comes with contentment,

And may the noose of strife and envy
Hang farther from your heart
Than the farthest star
From the deepest depth of the worlds' seas.

May you also nurse a child
That has opened the floodgate
Of another man's joy
As you have opened mine.

May the womb of your heart bring forth blessings for all time!

May you find favour with your *chi*[1],
And with the gods of our ancestors,
And with the Creator by whose providence
I shall name you for she whose loss
You have redeemed.

---

[1] *Chi*: personal god in Igbo cosmology.

A Note After Dark

Tonight I shall sleep and breathe gently,
More gently than I ever have;
I shall dream of your indivisible charms
Cradled in your soft, maternal arms.

Our daughter is all beauty tonight;
She lays like peace on a cushion of flowers;
Her skin radiates a golden lustre,
The colour of our future.

How the still butterfly wings of her
Breathing rise and fall,
Rise and fall in rhythm with her diaphragm,
As she lays beside the wand of sleep.

Hence, for your sake and hers,
And the dreams growing
In the womb of our hearts,
Fear shall no longer possess me.

Fire Report

(An experiment in poetic journalism)

Whom do we have to thank
For the fire that has just burnt down a bank
In our university,
And for our incredulity
That while it raged and flared
No fire engine stirred?

They said it was "a strange and voracious fire"
That "guzzled up the building like a funeral pyre,"
That "it moved from room to room,
As though with a fiery broom,
And swept out documents and ate them up,"
That "it even sat on a counter and drank tea from an enamel
    cup,
Having smashed into the strong room."

They said "it walked with a swagger, putting on airs,"
Like the one they saw last week at Student Affairs,
And wondered that it would also creep
Into the building while everyone was asleep,
And how it might have sedated the same guards who
By day are hardly far from view,
As they heckle folks like me -- and you.

They even said "the fire
Tried to walk on a sky wire
To an adjacent roof,
With a 'V' sign on its cloven right hoof."

They also said "it laughed like Arson,
That Graftology[1] student of Professor Blackson."

"It first broke the window glasses to let in the winds," they said,
"And then began this full, relentless raid."

Perhaps it is for the hype
That they also said "it even sat on a swivel chair
To smoke a pipe,
Its hands dovetailed over its thick, black hair."

They said "it even danced on the roof," that they saw it hold up
    a beer can
On which was inscribed: "TO RESTORE THE DIGNITY
OF MAN."[2]

---

[1] Graftology, my coinage, would mean the study of graft, if it were truly
a branch of learning.

[2] TO RESTORE … MAN: the motto of the University of Nigeria, in
whose Nsukka campus the fire incident occurred in October 2005.

A Prayer to Love

Please, love, do not restrict me.

Let me be an oak in whose far-flung boughs, heavy with leaves,
A vast association of ideas can find perch and succour.

Let me be a banyan whose roots stretch far into and across the
    earth,
Whose shade casts its mystic arms across wide expanses,
Whose tangled branches weave an infinite shade,
The pavilion of humanity.

Let me be an ocean now in calm and now roaring with tumults,
A continent of winds and waters,
A primordial endless bowl that teems with life and utility,
That feeds the sky with moisture,
The earth with rain.

Please, love, do not restrict me.

But let me take in my currents the blood and pus of this
    wounded world.
Let me swell with the sluice of its corrupted ways,
To give it back the health of purity.

Let my back be the anvil of the tireless Creator rather than a
    haven for backbiters.
Let it stand firm, arched high, beady with sweat at the hammer
    of the good Providence.
And please do not urge me to hate before I know, or know
    before I love.

Let me be like the sun whose pact ends with light,
The bright perennial torch of all the worlds,
The eternal terror of darkness.

O that you would that I remain a wild bird of the skies,
An aerial émigré, ranging over vast lands and distances,
Yet connecting with the earth by sky-bound trees,
And that you would approve of my flight,
My integral vision of earth and progress,
That spurns the boundary-marking laws of men.

Contemplating Alienism[1]

"Hypocrisy is the wheel on which society runs."

— Imoh Eshiet[2], a remark in class

The alien would brand us "savages"
For nursing customs we had known for ages;
And taught by him we would learn in turns
That it is "savage" to kill with knives, "civilized" with guns,
"Civilized" to drink ethanol, and "savage" to sip "illicit gin,[3]
Which leaves you with a brutish, wild grin."

In his wake we have mastered the murder
Of brother by spiteful brother,
Preferably with the gun, of course,
And become inheritors of Cain's curse[4].

Do we know the dangers
Of arrogance judging strangers
And how great will prove our follies
For replicating his censorious volleys?

---

[1] Alienism, my coinage, refers to the tendency to capitulate easily and uncritically to the influence of aliens.

[2] Imoh Eshiet: one of my lecturers at the University of Calabar.

[3] The British colonial administrators in Nigeria once banned the production of and trade in locally brewed gin, having branded it "illicit gin," whereupon possession of the commodity became an offence punishable by law, a measure apparently motivated by their desire to guarantee exclusive British export of the commodity to the colony.

[4] In the Bible God is said to have cursed Cain after he killed Abel, his brother, out of spite. See Genesis 4: 11-12.

I ponder Okija[1] with sorrows in my heart,
And her shrines soon to be torn apart
By our home-grown invaders
And culture raiders,
Men who will dredge a gutter
To find space for both baby and bathwater.

Hiroshima was the harvest of death that forced
A dead-end on the Holocaust,
Proving that even "evil" can serve the "good" end
Of those who prove to be its friend?

---

[1] Okija: a semi-rural community in south-eastern Nigeria where a raid in 2005 by a contingent of the Nigerian Police led to the "discovery" of some native shrines whose controversial contents were described as outrageous by some of the country's journalists.

A Luminous Invasion

The dawn, with rays as thick as broom
Sticks, has pierced through my gloom;
Her light stands guard in my living room.

Nor could I – night's poet – have sought
Her light and the warmth it has brought,
Yoked as I am to the melancholic thought.

Yet, each passing night and coming day,
I have wished it will never pass away,
That it lasts and stays with each unbending ray.

Yes, I have wished that this dawning light
Of our friendship ever glows in my sight,
And ever keeps at bay the gloom of night.

A Song for Charity

A light shines in the eyes of Charity;
It is green, I must say:
A mild dazzle of clarity,
With an emerald ray.

The clear, precious-stone light
Gently shoots a ray;
Does it throb in the dead of night
As it glows by day?

A smile supple, the luminous lips
Of her eyes flutter,
The pink meniscus of her finger tips,
Her skin of butter!

All night long
My soul stood still in the clarity
Of that light, my heart humming a song
For Charity.

A Portrait of a Seated Lady

Her hair is a braided crown;
Her nose is sharp, like an arrow;
Her eyes, like polished stones, are white and brown,
Her teeth as white as bone marrow.

Her hands, placed on a table before us,
End in unvarnished, clean nails,
Each tipped with a perfect meniscus
White with the whiteness of marble, or misty sails.

Her legs, moderately plump and hairy,
Are angled on the hard terrazzo floor;
Her demeanour is warm and airy;
Her pose suggests an open door.

She wears a perspectival smile
Of an evenly rippling broadband
And a gaze that shrinks the hazy mile
And knocks the paintbrush off my hand!

Her Algebra of Sacrifice

She said at last that "it wasn't rejection
But sacrifice." So that by sheer chance
Or discernment he might arrive at the equation:
Plus sacrifice minus rejection equals non-acceptance?
And what difference does it make that in her
Algebra of sacrifice the subtraction of rejection
Does not add up to acceptance? And would she care
To ponder that in the means and ends of affection
There can be no sacrifice without a victim:
Some bleating dark ram for some yawning altar,
Or a worthier beast who is seen like him
As duly bound to pass from love to slaughter?
Yet he has a heart that must not break
For love's sake, or give in to its ache.

The Poet Upbraids His Coy Heartthrob

O that I would have been honoured by you
For trivia, and had your ardent ears to call
My own, heedful like your mind and heart – two
Parts of you now seeming to flee beyond recall,
To flee from me as though from some cunning traitor,
And not one seeking your hand to some serious end
Of love and care, to make you my life's inheritor,
And take you truly for my wife and friend.
But how even with persistent feigned scorn the milk
Of the heart may congeal and the blood harden
In the veins of love; and to mind your trifling ilk
Grieving past their prime justifies my adding:
Time may seem to wait for the coy lady
Even as it hastens on, or is gone already.

An Ode to the Light of Joy

The dawn I longed to see has broken;
Its shell sprinkles light across the earth.
It's the dawn of which my Muse had spoken:
"Its rays shall bring you succour and rebirth."

Messenger, never tardy with the torch of cheer,
What glad tidings bring you to my heart?
What healthy titbits to my hungry ear?
What breath-divine to energize my art?

I laughed and shivered at the thought of this light,
This light of your cheer and grace and love;
I was pierced by thunderbolts of delight
To see its dawn ascend the miles above.

Woman, warmth, femineity, gift of the Gods
That saw through my longing human heart,
Joining at once the tips of their royal rods
To claim another mortal to their part.

Benediction

(To Womanhood)

Tall like the tree of life,
May the leaves of your beauty
Never fall
From season to season,
From year to year.
And if they should fall,
As all things that ripen
Must fall,
May they fall on grounds
Richer than you can wish,
To breed new beauties
Better than you can know.
And may their germs of health
Live from age to age, through
Countless years of saplings and of trees,
Flowering in and out of season, leafy, radiant,
Fruitful like their first maternal source.

Show Me a Sign

Uyi: Dr. Molokwu[1] spoke of you
As one might praise an apple that smells like a rose
Whose blossom, drenched in light and dew,
Is perfect pleasure to the eye and nose.

She might have called you a myth,
A smile that casts a spell,
A song whose powers lie beneath
A breath that can quench the fire of hell.

I, too, once knew an Uyi. She was
A rose garland hung on a full blue moon.
Much burden of glory passed with her pulse
When she slept in her beauty's June.

Please show me a sign that I
May know again to lift my eyes
To that uncharted region of the sky:
Where beauty leads the heart to Paradise.

---

[1] Dr. Esohe Molokwu: a Nigerian academic and administrator. The poem apostrophizes one of her protégés.

The Noon of *Quo Vadimus?*

Egrets are gathered on a silt
Island on the Benue[1]: twenty and five
Birds massed on a sand mound built
By the toil of receding waters; two more arrive,
Their bills dipped in silence to the hilt.

Quiet girds their slender necks like rings,
As bird by white bird stands stock still,
Their pensive moods cooped beneath closed wings
As they watch the near-dry river laze by like a rill
Whence hope stirs, though not a morsel springs.

Face by gaunt face, it's for them the noon of
Quo Vadimus?[2], as they stare vacantly
At a languid trail of water rough
With grit and mud, their necks wobbling intermittently,
Their gaze beyond its once-aquatic trough.

Twenty and seven birds down in desolate times,
And lost in thought, rise bird by bird
From the silt mound as if to the chimes
Of a distant bell, their frames curved, their calls weird,
As they make to fly to other climes.

---

[1] The Benue: see the third footnote on page 47.
[2] *Quo Vadimus?* (Latin): Where do we go?

Legend of the Python and the Beast

Deep is the purple flood
Where the sabre-toothed beast
Goes to drink, his eyes gorged with blood,
This dawn whose sky is the colour of yeast.

On this dawn of stacked dominoes
The end of the beast nears.
But nobody sees and nobody knows
Or hears even with pricked-up ears
As death creeps up to the beast on a python's belly,
Death as death's reticulate harbinger – silently.

Men assert *impossible* when they should say
We cannot. A beast they could not approach
Another beast is about to strangle, to slay,
And swallow as a fowl ingests a roach.

Who Next?

A. K. Dikibo[1],
You have been the next to fall
In our killing field of a democracy.

Yours was a nozzle-and-butt bashing of the head
By "robbers" – for that's what *he* called them.

Robbers who only take their victim's life!
Who robbed Bola Ige[2] only of his life,
And Harry Marshall[3],
And Victor Nwankwo[4].

How the wind of death blows chills down my spine,
As dog-meat turns the choicest meat for dogs.

All hail our carnassial democracy!

Who next?

---

[1] Chief A(minasoari) K(ala) Dikibo (?–2004) was killed on his way to a political meeting of Nigeria's ruling People's Democratic Party. He was a chieftain of the party at the time of his murder.

[2] Chief Bola Ige (1930–2001) was murdered as a serving Attorney General and Minister of Justice of Nigeria.

[3] Chief Harry Marshall (?–2003), a regional chieftain of the All Nigerian People's Party (ANPP), one of Nigeria's opposition parties, was shot dead in his home in the capital, Abuja, on March 5, 2003.

[4] Chief Victor Nwankwo (1942–2002) was murdered in the city of Enugu, in eastern Nigeria; he was then the Managing Director of Fourth Dimension Publishers, Enugu.

The Threat and the Reason

They want him dead;
They're waiting for his head;
Because he stood for the truth,
And called them evil and uncouth,
They want him dead.

They want him dead;
They're waiting for his head;
For daring to hold up the light
Against their reign of night,
They want him dead.

To a Nigerian Activist

"A brave dog does not fight till old age."

– An Igbo proverb

Cease to look longingly
At your sword
Leaning in its scabbard
On the wall.

The years that recompense good deeds
Shall see to yours.

The world often wears its cap
On its buttocks;
And in its ways with gratitude
Some great devotion has been crowned with thorns
Or acclaimed with a drink of hemlock.

Battles have been won though lost
And lost though seemingly won;
And the faith of the cross[1] is but a Phoenix
That rose from the ashes of a cold crucifixion.

Time shall pay their dues
Who have spilt the blood of innocents
And wrung tears from the hearts of doves.

When the plaudits start to ape a grumble,
And our footings start to drag and stumble,
And glory turns to face a younger age,
It's time to take a bow and leave the stage.

---

[1] The faith of the cross: Christianity.

Father and Child

Father enjoyed walking and so do I.
His feet
Loved the feel of the sandy street
Under an arched blue sky.

I remember riding on his shoulders,
High and stout like a mountain's boulders;
He must have walked twelve miles to Nkwo Ngwa[1],
Those wood stalls on the western fringe of town

Where the sweet damp smell of saw dust
Flying off the electric saws
Filled my nose. Could father have cared
For that smell as I still do?
Could he have remembered it ever after?

My back, like a wind-filled sail,
Billowed with pride throughout that journey,
As I sat astride and rode the stallion
Of his shoulders, his raised head
A guard against my fall.

Father now lies with his forefathers,
And I have a son whose name is father's.

---

[1] Nkwo Ngwa: a timber market in Aba, in eastern Nigeria.

The Fierce Guard

(To the Enugu Campus of the University of Nigeria:
On my first visit on July 31, 2004)

The lion at your gate is poised to pounce;
He has reared into the air,
His paws light on firm ground.

His claws are unsheathed,
His mane bristles with light,
And a fiery roar ascends his throat;
He is poised to pounce.

He is charged with the pride and the glory we have lost;
And woe betide those who in those days
Would stray towards his plinth with ignorance;
These days they all stomp by,
Bearding the fierce guard.

The Glory of Addis[1]

The glory of Addis stands to the sky;
It is studded with gems and brilliances;
It is tinged with the blackness of pure coffee
And fragrant with the spice of the rue[2] leaf.

It is an ageless glory;
It is the glory of the mother of Africa's pride;
It is the glory of the beauty of Africa's freedom;
It is a jewelled glory, a jewelled glory!

---

[1] Addis: short for Addis Ababa.
[2] Rue: the name of a plant with small scented green leaves widely used by Ethiopians as a traditional spice for coffee.

The Palm wine Ode

"They are totally unacquainted with strong or spirituous liquors, and their principal beverage is palm wine….When just drawn it is of a most delicious sweetness, but in a few days it acquires a tartish and more spirituous flavour, though I never saw anyone intoxicated by it."

— Olaudah Equiano, *Equiano's Travels*

(To be read until the fourth stanza, and then preferably sung)

In the open,
Under the half-light of a half-moon,
We sat and drank wine, and drank up
A huge gourd of foaming wine – palm wine!

The light of the half-moon bounced off the crystal foam
From our bamboo cups that brimmed and ran over
With wine – palm wine!

And the winds came and carried off the flakes of shining foam
As they fell from our cups of wine – palm wine!

And the winds carried off the foam flakes
That twinkled like fireflies
As they fell from our cups of wine – palm wine!

Did we get drunk? Or half-drunk? Or tipsy?
Did we go home giddy, to wind up in a stupor?
Did we find some shy tongues running loose with words?
How none of these was noticed – the night we drank palm wine.

Tapped before the sunrise, and secured through the day,
It was rich with freshness – the fridge had kept it so.
The ice-cold of the freezer ensured the yeasts were numb,
Until beneath the half-moon – the night we drank palm wine.

Meat was at the ready – salted, peppered, dried.
"He-goat meat," we called it. – It had a stubborn hide.
It lent itself to chewing, with all that taste of brine,
And washing down with pleasure – the night we drank palm
    wine.

Shared in equal measures, in bulging bamboo cups,
The liquid, white like moonlight, was emptied from the gourd,
And we all left contented, confessing one to all,
That it was worth the vigil – the night we drank palm wine!

Song of the Palm wine Ode

Words and Music by **Ikeogu Oke**

Arr. with accompaniments by **Jude Nwankwo**

Song of the Palm wine Ode

sun rise, and secured through the day, It was rich with fresh-ness · the fridge had kept it so. The ice-cold of the free-zer ___ en-sured the yeasts were numb, Un-til be-neath the half moon - the night we drank palm wine. Meat was at the rea-dy - sal ted, pep-pered,

Pno.

W. Bl.

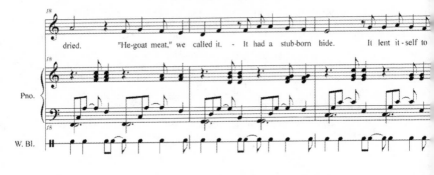

dried. "He-goat meat." we called it. - It had a stub-born hide. It lent it-self to

chew ing, with all that taste of brine, And wash ing down with pleasure - the night we drank palm

wine. Shared in e-qual mea-sures, in bulg-ing bam-boo cups, The li-quid, white like

Song of the Palm wine Ode

moon-light, was emp-tied from the gourd, And we all left con-ten-ted, con-fes-sing one to

all, That it was worth the vi-gil - the night we drank palm wine.

All Hail Our Alma Mater

All hail our Alma Mater!
American University of Nigeria,
Cradle of great achievers,
All hail! All hail! All hail!

Chorus: Set in the Sunny Valley,
        Among the Yola Plains,
        All hail our Alma Mater,
        Where good shall ever reign.

A vision built on solid grounds,
A rare bequest for knowledge,
To raise the youth of Africa
To lead from age to age.

All hail our Alma Mater!
American University of Nigeria,
Whence the light of learning
Shall ever warm the earth.

All Hail Our Alma Mater

Words and Music by **Ikeogu Oke**
Arr. for S.A.T.B. by **Jude Nwankwo**

All Hail Our Alma Mater

raise the youth of A - fri - ca To lead from age to age._____ All hail o[u]

Al - ma Ma - ter! A - me-ri-can U-ni - ver-si-ty of Ni - ge - ria, Whence th[e]

light of learn - ing Shall e - ver warm the earth._____

A Sailor's Monologue

*Your boss – need I state his name? – is one of the monarchs of
  our Nigerian skies:
Has the eagle become so weak and hungry that it must now learn
  to catch flies?[1]*

I ride the crest of my thirty-eighth year!
Tempest-tossed, yet I know no fear.
Nor has it dulled my sense of mission
That I am through with Fourth Dimension.

Theirs – a shore whence I must set sail;
I may whimper, but I shall not wail.
They strain the aqueous world in which we live
And worsen their woes who look back and grieve.

My Muse and I – we are creatures of hope;
Vast is this sea, more vast its inner scope.
Sailors with faith, passion and truth,
Our oars tame the roaring waves of youth.

These storms shall learn to leave our craft at rest,
The while we learn to rule our endless quest.
Nor shall it ever dull our sense of mission,
That we are through with Fourth Dimension.

---

[1] The couplet was originally part of a letter of which the poem was an
epilogue; the (second) line alludes to the Arabic proverb: "An eagle does
not catch flies."

A Question of Tactics

"One can only fight fire with fire."[1]

– Nelson Mandela

Should we fight fire
With fire
Or with water?

Should we return
A slap
For a slap
Or turn
The other cheek?

Should we love
Or hate
Our enemies
Or do good
Or ill
To those who
Despitefully
Use us?

It's a question
Of tactics: each oppression
Makes its own
Demands,
And fights
Whatever move
To end its reign.

---

[1] Quoted by Matthew Page in the Letters section of *Prospects*, a British journal, for June 2004. The quote is on page 4 of the publication.

A Reply

Dear Madam,
Your letter says I must quit
Or leave you no choice but to evict,
To flush me out "like Saddam.[1]"
But, Madam,
Does this read like a script from Saddam,
Written in his glory days,
When he seemed fixed in his curious ways,
Unable to see that when tyrannies tumble
By tyrannies no one ever cares to heed their grumble?

You give me just one day – the shortest in history –
To comply with this order from Madam Peremptory –
Or find my four limbs scattered to your winds:
My arms to your headwinds? My legs to your whirlwinds?

Mistress of the winds, mistress of the winds,
And how the rumble of your rage unwinds!

That dawn of my eviction is already here;
But your agents shall come and not find a cornered bear;
And if I leave – yes, if I leave –
I shall not grieve.

---

[1] Saddam Hussein (1937-2007): a former Iraqi President.

A Worker's Quandary

(To J. Elspeth Smith[1])

If we easily take a plunge into the abyss,
I would be gone with this dusk or by dawn,
Done with these threats to "fire" and "dismiss"
(And these schemes to make me love to fawn),
As if a boss is just a nozzle or a trigger
Or perhaps a mere wave of the hand
By a taskmaster and a constant intriguer
Who loves to wield the stick of reprimand
For wrongs no eye can see or mind fathom.
How to work becomes to risk enslavement,
To wear a wild grin before the irksome,
And sham the smell of scent from excrement.
O that I could flee this job-disease
With a rash plunge into the abyss!

---

[1] J. Elspeth Smith: an American administrator and head of the University Relations Department of the American University of Nigeria, Yola.

Nsukka – December 2007

The rains have retreated into a farther sky.
The hills are brown-baked with sunlight.
The winds – noisy with squalls and dry –
Force their drearier aspects on our plight.

These – I am told – are the days when a season
Draws his fiery chariot up the hills,
Obscured now and then by plumes of dust.

These – I have seen – are the days when a season
Draws his wagon up the sun-baked hills,
Obscured now and then by plumes of smoke.

And how the once-brown grass
On the hills
Is charred
In his wake!

Pruning?

What tree,
Its trunk deeply scarred,
Its branches lopped off,
Scattered
On the ground
Like
Frozen limbs!

You and I

An evening. Almost dusk. You and I. Promenading.
Taking a walk to a pub as the night was descending.

And darkness rolled down the skies
And hung in sable sheets before us.
And fear had tipped her finger on my pulse.

And I was musing. Not on love.
Though love became the reason we were there.
Not on the stellar multitudes above.
Nor the moon whose radiance charmed the air.

My mind was playing host to stranger thoughts.
Of the sourness of vinegar.
Of the canker in the apple's core.
Of oysters. Irritations. Gems!
Oceanic wastes of water to the thirst.
Yes, of paradoxes. Quirks. Ironies.
Such nameless twists of fate
That took us there.
You and I. Twin imperfections.

I would lift up my eyes and would not see.
I would think back and would not remember.
My gaze upraised would know no cheer
Save you were at my side – solace!

And if you will reckon with it:
A stick must split to make a catapult.
And that's a weapon to propel a stone.
Nor can two legs support a pot
In the firm manner of a tripod.

So we'll find a worthy friend besides.
Perhaps a friend within, in the midst of us.
For three is the perfection of unity.

Now I'm alone.
The room is getting darker with the night.
The caravan of my thoughts marches to strange destinations,
With the sunny radiance of your smile.

My Father and I

> "Every man's death begins with the death of his father."
>
> – Orhan Pamuk[1]

The day my father died I died a little – and began
My final descent to the grave.

He shall resurrect the day I die – the day I reach the grave.
The ship of my dreams shall bring him back to life,
Riding the crest of a distant wave.

And we shall meet
Eye to eye,
Father to son,
Face to face
And ghost to ghost.

And the whirlwind of our entwined bodies
Shall swirl down the shore of this life,
The wind of a new death and a wind ancestral,
The whirlwind of proof that dying makes a man,
The whirlwind of my father and I.

---

[1] Orhan Pamuk: a Turkish novelist and essayist; he was awarded the 2006
Nobel Prize in literature. The preceding quote is from a review of Mr.
Pamuk's *Other Colours* (a collection of essays) by Percy Zvomuya, published
on page 36 of the May 2008 edition of *words etc*, a South African journal.

A Mentor and His Protégé

A prophet, mounting the heavens
Of eminence, dropped
His mentor's mantle
Down the wind.

His protégé, picking up
The holy cloth,
Smirched it with a curse.

O that the urchins
Mocked his hairless[1] pate!
O that he smudged
The cloth
By cursing them!

---

[1] Hairless: bald.

A Partner in Progress

(An Anthem[1] for Shell Nigeria)

The Shell Petroleum Development Company
Is a light that shines out to many,
A light on which you surely can depend,
The beacon of a true and worthy friend.

In Nigeria, we've been here since the work began,
Putting in the best we ever can,
In rain or shine, by night and day,
To make the nation greater all the way.

---

[1] The anthem, originally conceived as a poem, was commissioned by an affiliate of the Shell Petroleum Development Company of Nigeria to be written from the standpoint of a corporate mouthpiece.

A Partner in Progress
(An Anthem for Shell Nigeria)

Words and Music by **Ikeogu Oke**
Arr. for S.A.T.B. by **Jude Nwankwo**

Moderato

The Shell Pet-ro-leum De-ve-lop-ment Com-pa-ny Is a light that shines out to ma-ny, A light on which you sure-ly can de-pend, The bea-con of a true and wor-thy friend. In Ni-ge-ria, we've been here since the work be-gan, Put-ting in the best we e-ver can, In rain or shine, by night and day, To make the na-tion great-er all the way.

Song of the Gathering Guests

(To the city of Calabar)

Jewel city set amid deep waters!
We have come – sojourners from far places –
Travellers by land and air and sea –
Guests drawn by peace to your quiet shores –
To drink the nectar of your tenderness.

We have come –
Pilgrims for the peace that falls like dewdrops
From your gentle skies;
O, jewel city, receive us!

We have come for the warmth of that embrace
Whose legend has enriched the pride of distant lands;
Now, throw open your arms,
Lay bare your chest and, jewel city, receive us!

Receive us – even as your streets widen
Under the wand of Donald[1] –
And his gracious care refines your charms – receive us!

O city – whose guests are now escorted
By a phalanx of trees – whose green lawns
Excite the appetite – whose street lights
Are now soaring into a blue sky –
Lights whose beams are a shower of golden rays –
Whose wings are wide like the eagle's – receive us!

---

[1] Donald: Mr. Donald Duke, a former Governor of Cross River State of which Calabar is the capital.

How time must desert us though we care for her –
Wanton maid and mistress – how she must desert us!
How she must go wandering into other arms –
Better lovers perhaps –
How she may even now quickly desert us
Unless – jewel city – you are kind to receive us!

We come – waiters on your wide wings – tourists even –
Our lips rustling with prayers –
Our hearts laden with bouquets of goodwill;
We come – muttering prayers
That your peace may endure the brusqueness of wild seasons –
That your beauty may not wane with time –
That progress may not taint your innocence.

For what is peace if roughened by some clime?
Or beauty if its charm must fade with time?
Or progress if its dawn must break with crime?

Unity Poems

Circulating Good

Ripples of thought
Of infinite good
Radiate forth
From my mind
Transversely travelling
Through all universe
Cleansing all things
Wholly bright.
My infinite thoughts
Of perfect good
Permeate horizons,
Cross all boundaries,
Break through all limitations
Delivering good to all,
And longitudinally
They are reflected to me
With folds of good
Multiplied
Regenerating me.

Inspired by Light

Bright, shining candle;
Ever cheerful, warm,
Aglow, effulgent, smiling
And impersonal.
You take full form;
Stick of wax, and wick,
And tongue of light
With radiant halo;
And dispel all gloom
With your selfless light.
You live to serve;
Active, untiring,
Multiplying your manifest good;
And in so brief a life,
Fill our own lives
With invaluable lessons
In Godliness.

From Now

Free on an open road
In an open world,
The past
Stretched behind me
In trodden ways,
A cheerful future
Lures my eager feet:
Standing in this material
Time – this moment – now!
I dwell no more
On the past,
Cavil no more,
Forebode not again of things to come,
I let go of all and let God,
And leave all guidance
To the voice within,
As I surely move
To meet my good
From now.

Gratitude

For faith and strength
To sow the earth with seed,
For fertile showers
And for fostering light,
For calm to watch
Our seedlings sprout and grow,
And oh for seasons
Pleasant in their roles,
And wind-breath gentle
On our verdant fields,
And, Lord, for harvest
Rich from lavish earth,
And all the goodness
That bespeak your care;
We, your blessed children,
Proffer thanks.

That's the Time

That's the time –
When the answer
Lies beyond your grasp,
And all your human wisdom
Seems a null.

That's the time –
When the tangled ways
Resist your mind,
And thought's great river
Seems forever dammed.

That's the time –
When the one true end
Remains unfound,
And all your searching
Seems to fail for good.

That's the time
To come apart awhile
And take good counsel
From the voice within.

Like Sailors

There is no end to our horizons:
The sea in endless
Expanse meets the sky.
And we like sailors
Mount and ride
The waves,
And onward sail
In vast eternities.
The broad and endless heavens
Stretch above,
Like the water
Bright and blue below.
And we like sailors
Mount the buoyant waves,
And onward voyage
In eternal good.

Beacons

Lights in the darkness shining,
Pleasant in your aerial majesty:
Moon and bright stars
Of the endless sky.
Oh, broad and vast
And sparkling guides
Of vision, life, and faith –
What a service
In your pleasantness!
To project light
And hope in darkness
And in all despair
And complement the sun
That brightens yet
The time of day.

Yellow Beauty

Skywards,
A tree stretches
Her long arms
Swathed in yellow leaves
In a blithe autumnal gesture:
Leaves, luxuriant arms,
Flung in their yellow grace
Towards the sky!
And I who watch
Her arms
Amid the sky,
Her yellow beauty
In assured display,
May I not revel
And grasp the sky,
Though my leaves
Are soon to fall away?

Mountaineer

You grip the crags
With bold, tenacious hands,
And rise towards
The mountain's jutted peak,
Brave one heedless
Yet of all despair,
Straining closer
To your goal with faith,
Ever strong
And ever holding fast.
Look down and tell
The ones that come below:
How high from ground
The strength of faith can rise,
What great endurance
Mounts the rocky heights!

Open Door

I walk through
An open door,
Leave it open,
Then hear a murmur:
Why not shut the door?

Walk through an open door?
And then shut it?
An open door?

A Cocktail of Epigrams

Epigram on a Remark by Charles E. Nnolim[1]

Fame from wealth and power departs with wealth and power;
Fame from art and virtue endures the eternal hour.

Epigram Anticipating a Pan-African Epic

Speak, poet, that the truth may be known and in the end prevail
    against falsehood,
And that the force of evil may lie low, vanquished by the force
    of good.

Epigram on the Eruption of "Xenophobic" Attacks in South Africa

Those "xenophobes" may have a case, and one that's strong,
But a wrong is never used to right a wrong;
For a wrong that's used to set a wrong aright
Is more than apt to bring two wrongs to light.

Epigram on the Unmasking of a False Mentor

Fools, thinking they can see tomorrow,
Ignore today the wrongful paths they follow,
Ignore as well the shadows cast
By their dark and crooked past.

But fate awaits the proper time and place
To tear the mask of pretence off their face,
To rip the veil of pretence off their back;
She's stripped this "healer" to reveal a quack!

---

[1] Charles E. Nnolim: see the first footnote on page 52.

Epigram to *Things Fall Apart*

Among earth's Himalayan books soars your shimmering peaks;
Above the muffled din of the arts your eternal voice speaks.

A "Democracy Day" Epigram

(On the Theme of "Snatching Defeat from the Jaws of Victory"[1])

Wake up, Mr. President, from your droning slumber,
And bring a new dawn to our teeming number:
Nigeria crawls like a millipede
Towards hopes ever wont to recede.

Epigram in Support of Bassey Ekpo Bassey[2] as Obong of Calabar

There are not many such Basseys
Roundly loved by the Efik masses;
Nor was there ever such a worthy sovereign
To show the Efik what it means to reign.

Epigram on the Nigerian Tiger

(To Nuhu Ribadu[3])

Our nation's tiger is a curious beast
That loves to indulge the unwary activist:
His ride on it is often brisk and gay;
The ride elapsed, the rider turns its prey.

---

[1] An expression coined by Chinua Achebe in *The Trouble with Nigeria*.
[2] Bassey Ekpo Bassey: a Nigerian intellectual, politician and reform activist.
[3] Nuhu Ribadu: a former Chairman of Nigeria's Economic and Financial Crimes Commission (EFCC).